Rabbit and Owl lived in a big, old oak tree. They loved their huge old tree. It made them feel safe and warm. They slept all day in the warm, cosy tree.

When night came Owl would wake up. He would open his eyes as wide as saucers. He loved to see the stars and moon twinkle in the night sky.

Every night Owl would fly down to see Rabbit. Every night Rabbit would wait for Owl. Then they would talk all night long. They had been very best friends for years.

READ

Read pages 6 to 9

Purpose: To find out what happened one night when Owl went to see Rabbit.

EXPLORE

Pause at page 9

What happened when Owl went to see Rabbit? How was Rabbit feeling? How do you think Owl felt?

What did Owl do on page 9? Why do you think the sentences are repeated like this? What is Owl's hooting compared to? (*fire engine, ambulance*)

What do you think is the matter with Rabbit?

Look at page 6. Find the words that Owl spoke. What did he say? How do you know? (*identify speech marks*)

Tricky word (page 6):
The word 'answer' may be beyond the children's word recognition skills. Tell this word to the children.

4

One night Owl woke up and went to see Rabbit, but Rabbit wasn't there!
Owl called, "Hello, Rabbit." But Rabbit didn't answer.
Owl called again, "Rabbit! Rabbit! Where are you?"
6
Rabbit still didn't answer, so Owl went into Rabbit's burrow. Rabbit was there alone.
"Rabbit? Are you OK?" asked Owl. But Rabbit still didn't answer.

"Rabbit, my old friend, answer me," said Owl. But Rabbit didn't answer. He just looked down. Owl thought Rabbit looked very, very sad indeed.
8
Whooooo
So Owl hooted loudly.
He hooted like a fire engine.
He hooted like an ambulance.
He hooted like an owl who wants his friend to smile.

Read pages 10 to 13

READ

Purpose: To find out why Rabbit was so sad.

Pause at page 13

EXPLORE

What was the matter with Rabbit? How did he feel? How do you think Owl felt? What did Owl do about it?

What does Rabbit say on page 11? How do you know he is speaking? (*identify speech marks*)

What is special about the word 'today'? Why is it written in bold? Let's read it again together with expression.

Look at Rabbit's speech on page 12. Which words do we need to emphasise? Ask a child to read aloud with expression and emphasis.

Please turn to page 14 for Revisit and Respond activities.

Rabbit still didn't smile.
"What's the matter?" said Owl.
Rabbit still didn't answer.
"What's the matter, my old friend?"
asked Owl.

10

"Owl, I am not **old**. I am eight,"
said Rabbit.
Owl didn't know what to say.
"I am eight," said Rabbit again.
"I am eight **today**."
Then Owl **did** know what to say.
"Happy Birthday, Rabbit!" said Owl.

11

Rabbit still looked sad.
"Today is my birthday," he said,
"but no one has remembered.
No one has **ever** remembered.
I have never had a
real birthday."

12

Owl didn't know what to say,
and he didn't know what to do.
He needed to think but he could
only think his best thoughts on his
thinking branch at the top of the tree.
So he flew up to his thinking branch.

13

LESSON 2

RECAP

Recap lesson 1

What has happened so far?

What was Rabbit's problem?

Where did Owl go and why?

What do you think Owl will do to cheer Rabbit up?

READ

Read pages 14 to 17

Purpose: To find out about Owl's good idea and what he did about it.

EXPLORE

Pause at page 17

What was Owl's bright idea? What did he do about it? How do you think he feels? How do you think Rabbit will feel?

Where is the party going to be? Find the sentence that tells you. Why was this a good place?

Look at page 14. Why are there dots between 'thought' and 'birthday card'? This is because Owl is pausing. The dots are called ellipses. It means we are waiting for something to come next. Ask the children to read this passage, pausing at the dots.

Owl thought very hard.
"What is a **real** birthday?"
And then his best thoughts came.
He thought . . . birthday card.
He thought . . . birthday present.

And then his thoughts came faster and faster.
Birthday party!
Birthday games!
Birthday cake!

Then he had an even better thought. *Birthday cabbage!* Rabbit loved cabbage, and they could have the party in the garden with the big cabbage.

Owl flew to his hole as fast as he could.
He wrote birthday invitations as fast as he could.

Then he gave out the invitations as fast as he could.

Read pages 18 to 21

Purpose: To find out who came to Rabbit's party and what they did.

Pause at page 21

Who was at the party?

How did Rabbit feel? What words tell you this? (*Thank you! Thank you!*)

What was Bat's special present for Rabbit?

What did they have instead of a birthday cake? Why?

Point out the speech marks on page 21. Choose children to be Rabbit, Owl and Badger and ask them to read out the spoken words. Another child can be the narrator.

Find the word 'night' on page 19. Can you find another word with this spelling pattern on page 20? (*light*)

Then Owl flew down to the garden
with the big cabbage. The stars lit up
the cabbage patch.
"What a **lovely** place for a party,"
said Owl.

Then Owl flew to Rabbit's burrow.
"Rabbit!" he cried, "Come out!"
Rabbit came out. He looked startled.
"Follow me, quickly!" cried Owl.
So they raced off into the moonlit night.

Fox, Badger, Squirrel and Bat were
in the garden.
"Happy Birthday!"
"Happy Birthday, Rabbit!"
"Eight today!"
They all had birthday presents for
Rabbit. Bat even gave him a flying
display! Bat flew upside down in the
light of the moon.
"Wonderful!" thought Owl.

"Thank you! Thank you!" said Rabbit.
"What next?" he asked.
"Birthday party games?" asked Owl.
So they played Hopscotch and Pass
the Carrot.

"Thank you! Thank you!" said Rabbit.
"What next?" he asked.
"Birthday cake?" asked Badger.
"Birthday **cabbage**!" said Owl.

Read pages 22 to the end

Purpose: To find out what Rabbit did and how he felt at the end of the story.

Pause at page 24

What did Rabbit do when he blew out the candle? What do you think he wished for?

How did Rabbit feel at the end? Which sentence tells us this?

Which words are emboldened on page 24? Choose two children to read this page aloud as Owl and Rabbit, using appropriate expression and emphasising the words in bold.

He lit the candle and
everybody sang . . .

Then Rabbit blew out the candle.
"You must make a birthday wish," said Owl.
"What could I wish for?" asked Rabbit. He
gave lots of little jumps and one big one.
"You could wish for a slice of birthday
cabbage," said Owl.

Later, Owl and Rabbit talked all night.
"Well, Rabbit," said Owl. "Was it a **real**
birthday?"
"Oh yes," said Rabbit. "It was
a **very** real birthday. Thank you
so much, Owl."

After Reading

Revisit and Respond

Lesson 1

- Ask the children in pairs to take the part of Rabbit and Owl, and role-play the story so far.

- Ask them to think of some sentences that Rabbit and Owl might have said to each other. Write these out in full on the board and ask children to put speech marks in the correct place.

- Ask them to brainstorm a list of words to describe how Rabbit was feeling and also how Owl was feeling at different stages in the book. Write them on the board under headings 'Owl' and 'Rabbit'.

Lesson 2

- Ask the children to retell the story to a partner, expressing their own views about the characters.

- Ask the children to choose their favourite part of the story and give reasons for this.

- Using a picture of Owl and Rabbit, write a conversation Owl and Rabbit might have (teacher scribing). Rewrite as a dialogue using speechmarks.

- Ask the children to generate 'ight' words, e.g. sight, fight, light, night, might, slight, right, tight. Ask them to list these on individual whiteboards.

Follow-up
Independent Group Activity Work

This book is accompanied by two photocopy masters, one with a reading focus, and one with a writing focus, which support the teaching objectives of this book. The photocopy masters can be found in the Planning and Assessment Guide.

PCM F5.1 (*reading*)

PCM F5.2 (*writing*)

You may also like to invite the children to read the text again, during their independent reading (either at school or at home).

Writing

Guided writing: Write a book review of this story using the writing frame on PCM F5.2

Extended writing: Write a story about what might happen if your friends and family forgot your birthday or a big day you were looking forward to (e.g. Christmas, Diwali etc.).

Assessment Points

Assess that the children have learnt the main teaching points of the book by checking that they can:

- engage with books through exploring and enacting interpretations (e.g. children take the parts of the main characters and act out the story).